Usborne
First Sticker Book
Christmas

Illustrated by Katya Longhi
Words by Alice Beecham
Designed by Keith Newell

You'll find all the stickers at the back of the book.

Christmas Town

Hidden in a snowy valley near the North Pole is a busy little place called Christmas Town, where Santa Claus and his elves live. Stick on some more buildings to finish the town.

Sleigh

Mail

Ice Rink

Santa's Workshop

All across Christmas Town, you can hear the tapping and clinking of tiny tools coming from Santa's Workshop. Fill the scene with elves making and painting toys.

The stables

Santa wouldn't be able to travel far without the help of his reindeer. Add some more reindeer to the scene and some busy elves looking after them.

Dasher

Comet

Vixen

Cupid

Donner

Blitzen

7

Christmas baking

In Santa's Bakery, a warm, spicy scent is wafting through the air. There are cookies to ice, gingerbread houses to decorate, and all kinds of cakes and pies to make. Which festive treat do you like best?

Dec 23

Decorating the tree

These elves are decorating the Christmas tree in the town square.
Stick lots of bright and shiny decorations on the branches, then
fill the rest of the square with cheery elves singing carols.

Christmas Eve

Santa is getting ready to deliver all the presents. He'd better get going. There are lots of houses to visit by morning. Stick on the rest of the reindeer and a few more elves and presents, too.

Delivering presents

While everyone is fast asleep, Santa and a few lucky elves visit all the homes. Very quietly, they bring in all the Christmas presents. Stick some more presents next to the tree.

Christmas Day

With all the gifts delivered, it's time to celebrate. Stick some musicians on the stage, then fill the page with elves, reindeer, and Santa Claus himself.